Courtesy Rules!
By Lewena Bayer

©Civility Experts Inc. Worldwide
All Rights Reserved 2020

Introduction
I'm Proud of Being Me!

Respect, respect, respect, everyone is talking respect. What is respect? That's right, respect is all about showing care and consideration for others. Practicing good manners is one way to show respect because manners are rules for how to be nice to each other. There's someone else you have to show respect for too. And who's that? It's you! In this book, we're going to learn that it's also important to respect ourselves.

Did you ever hear someone say, "Be good to yourself?" Well, there are lots of ways to be good to yourself and we're going to learn all about them. Showing care and consideration for yourself is called "self-respect".

Other people are important, but it's easier to show care and consideration for someone else if you know how to take care of yourself first. This is important because how you look and act on the outside shows other people how you feel about yourself on the inside.

Can you guess how to show self-respect? If you guessed by staying neat and clean and trying to be positive and friendly to people, you're right! But there are other ways too. The way you stand or walk, the way you behave in public places, and the way you talk to people are all important. Most importantly, be proud to be who you are! Show respect for others but don't forget to show care and consideration for yourself too. When you wake up every day, you can remind yourself about self-respect by saying out loud: "Today I'll be polite to me and show the world I'm proud to be."

Chapter 1
First Things First: Take Care of Me!

We all know that manners are about showing care and consideration for others, right? This is very important because respecting each other helps us all live together and be friends. But it's very difficult to take care of others if we don't take care of ourselves first. We're all different but we're all special too. It's important to know a little about ourselves and what makes us special so that we can understand how other people are different and special in their own way.

It's What's Inside That Counts

Have a look in the mirror. Smile a big smile at yourself and say out loud three things that you can see "on the outside" that make you look different from everybody else in the world. Here are some hints. Maybe you're tall, maybe you have really nice white teeth, or maybe lots of curly hair. Think about what "outside" things make you look different from all your friends. These things make you special.

There are also other things that make you extra special, things on the "inside." These are the things that people can't see or know about you just by looking at you. Maybe these are things that you're good at. Is there something you do really well? Maybe you're really good at mathematics, maybe you take really good care of your little brother or sister, or maybe you are really good at making other people laugh. If you take your time and really think about it, you will probably think of at least ten things that make you special and proud of being who you are.

Write down a list of ten things about yourself that are special on the inside. Put this list up beside your mirror so you can remind yourself what makes you special. Remember, just like you have special things about you, other people have special things about them too!

Everyone Is Special
When you meet other people, try to see what makes them special. Show respect for what makes them different from you and don't forget, they have "inside" things that make them extra special, maybe you just can't see them.

If other people see that you respect them, maybe they will show respect for you. And, if they see how proud you are to be you, maybe they will feel proud of themselves too. Don't forget, it's what's inside that counts the most!

Do this exercise with a friend, parent, or teacher. Take the list you wrote about yourself. Now you and your friend each write down ten things you think are special about each other. Compare your friend's list to your own. Did they see the same special things about you that you wrote down about yourself? Did they see different things?

Isn't it great that other people can see special things about you? More importantly, you can seep special things about them too. That's because we all have things that make us proud to be who we are, on the outside, and on the inside.

No-One is Perfect
So now we know that everyone is special and that we all have something we do better than anyone else. We also know that what makes each of us special is that we're different from each other and so we try to show respect for the differences. We all can't be good

at everything, right? If we were, we'd be perfect, and nobody's perfect! No matter how special we are, everyone makes mistakes. No matter how good we are at some things, there are other things we don't do as well as our friends and classmates. It's important to remember that we are not perfect and that we will sometimes make mistakes. Do don't feel too bad when you do! And, please don't be hard on the other people when they make mistakes. We know that we're not perfect, so we do not put pressure on others to be perfect either.

When we respect who we are, and know that we are not perfect, we have confidence. Confidence means we are not afraid to be ourselves and we feel proud to be who we are. Having self-respect also means that even though we know that we may never be perfect, we want to be the best we can be, so we always try to improve.

Being the Best We Can Be!
So, now that we know there are "inside" things that we do well and that makes us special, we want to make sure to keep feeling good on the inside.

How do you think we can do that? Well, did you ever hear someone say, "You are what you eat?" This is a way of saying that if you eat healthy food, you'll be a healthy person – you'll feel good on the inside. If you eat only snack foods or "junk food" and no fruits and vegetables, you won't feel very good. Eating healthy and being sure to get lots of exercise and fresh air is one way to show and care and consideration for yourself. It's also important to get lots of sleep. It's not very easy to be nice to ourselves or show consideration for other people if we are tired and grouchy. Here's something you can do to see if you are taking good care of yourself.

Every day look at the list below and remind yourself to do these healthy things.

1. Eat some fruits and vegetables.
2. Drink lots of water, at least six glasses a day.
3. Don't have too many treats like chips, soda pop, or candies.
4. Get some exercise every day.
5. Go outside and enjoy the fresh air.
6. Get a good night's sleep.

If you try to do all of these things every day, you will feel really good on the inside and this will show on the outside.

Meet Spiffy Same and Sloppy Sue
Maybe this is a good time for you to meet two of my favourite friends. Both are special in their own way; they are fantastically fun and very friendly. There is only one difference between them, Spiffy Sam is careful to be polite to himself, but Sloppy Sue is not.

Here is an ordinary day for Sloppy Sue. She sleeps in late then gets up on the wrong side of the bed. She throws on yesterday's dirty wrinkled clothes and stomps downstairs. She eats potato chips and soda pop for breakfast – better that than nothing, she thinks to herself. Sloppy Sue doesn't bother to comb her hair or brush her teeth. Sometimes she doesn't even wash her face all day or take a bath all week. Sloppy Sue is not the most popular at school because other people think she looks sloppy, tired, and even a little grouchy.

Spiffy Sam behaves much differently. His alarm clock goes off and he jumps out of bed, bright-eyed and bushy-tailed. He puts on a clean, ironed T-shirt and his favourite blue shorts. Then he goes to the bathroom and washes his hands and face. Sam's favourite breakfast is a peanut butter and banana sandwich with a big glass of milk. After breakfast, Sam helps clean up the table and runs upstairs to brush his teeth so he'll have a fresh breath all day. Spiffy Sam feels great. Everyone he meets can see it by his smile and everyone wants to hang out with him.

See what a difference being polite to yourself makes? Throughout the next chapters, we'll check in on Spiffy Sam and Sloppy Sue and see how they handle the challenges of being respectful to themselves in different situations.

Well, what have we learned so far? Let's see, what would Spiffy Sam say about being polite to yourself? Hmmmm?

1. Showing care and consideration for yourself is called self-respect.
2. Everyone is special and we're all different. It's what's inside that counts and we should feel proud of who we are.
3. No-one is perfect. We can't expect ourselves to be, and we can't expect other people to be perfect either.
4. We need to eat healthy foods and take care of ourselves, so we feel good on the inside because
5. it's important to be the best you can be.

Do you think Sloppy Sue remembers all these things?

Chapter 2
Ready to Go, Head to Toe: Rules for Grooming

Remember how we said that how you look on the outside tells other people how you feel on the inside? Well, one thing we do when we feel good about ourselves is make sure that we look good from head to toe. This is called grooming. Grooming is a very big job that takes time and energy. We have to take care of our hair, teeth, skin, hands, and our nails. Let's start with hair.

Hair Today, Gone Tomorrow!
Have you ever heard someone being called a "mop-top"? This is a way of telling someone that their hair is too long or dirty or that it looks messy.

Since the first thing that people will see is your face, it's important to keep your hair neat and clean so your smiling happy face – not your messy, dirty hair – can be seen! So, remember to wash your hair every time you shower or bath. And if your hair is long, keep it tied back or wear barrettes when you are around other people.

What if you're wearing a hat? Then you don't have to worry that your hair is neat and clean, right? Wrong! You should only wear your hat when you're outside – not in the house and never at the dinner table.

When you take your hat off, you might get something called "hat head" where your hair is all smushed down and messy, so if you're going to wear a hat, bring a comb with you so you can fix your hair up. Another important thing to remember about hats is to wear them properly. Backwards, sideways, even upside down, a hat that isn't sitting properly just looks sloppy.

One other thing to remember is not to play with your hair, spin it around your fingers, or chew on it. It doesn't look very nice and it's not very healthy. Sloppy Sue once twisted her hair so often that she couldn't get her finger untangled. Spiffy Sam had to help her and teach to her that twisting, twirling, and swirling your hair will get it tangled – and it'll hurt a lot when you have to comb it out later!

Right in the Teeth

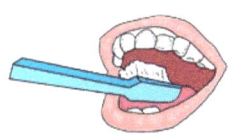

If people are backing away as you're talking, waving a hand in front of their face, or sticking a clothespin on their nose, they are probably trying to tell you that you have bad breath.

There's only one way to keep bad breath away and that is to keep your teeth clean. Brush your teeth as often as you can. You should always brush in the morning and at night, but it's even better if you can brush after every meal.

Flossing is important too. Next time you go to the dentist, ask them to show you how to use dental floss. It is a thin piece of string that is coated with wax. When you floss your teeth, you can get out all the tiny bits of food that get stuck between your teeth and sometimes cause bad breath. Another thing to remember, is to make sure to check in the mirror now and then to make sure there's nothing stuck in your teeth.

Even if you brush your teeth as much as possible, you should still take care to check your breath when you get up in the morning, after you eat spicy foods, or if your mouth feels dry. Sometimes it's a good idea to carry small mints with you just in case you need to freshen your breath. Chewing gum helps too, but there are special rules to gum chewing.

Did you ever sit beside someone who was chewing gum? Some people chew with their mouth open and blow big bubbles that pop on their face.

Chewing gum is not really a very polite habit. It is sometimes noisy and when we're chewing, we don't realize that we're making noises or that our mouth is open. If you are worried about fresh breath, have a peppermint instead, and if you do chew gum, put it in the garbage when you want to have a conversation with someone.

Hands Down!
Good for you! You are certainly learning quickly. With all this confidence and self-respect, you're going to be meeting a lot of new people and shaking their hands when you say hello. With all that handshaking going on, it will be very important to keep your hands and nails clean. It would be terrible if you went to shake hands and your fingernails were full of mud from playing outside or if you were covered in paint from doing crafts at school. Even worse, what if you just had lunch and there was mustard on your fingers? You wouldn't make a very good first impression if you shook hands and got mustard all over someone.

It's important to always remember to wash your hands after meals, after you've been playing outside, after you've used the washroom, and any time they are dirty. Remember to check your hands every once in a while to see that they are clean. It's also important to use a napkin when you eat and to keep a cloth handy when you are doing painting and other messy crafts.

Nailing It!
Keeping your fingernails clean and neat is another important way to show people that you respect yourself. The most important way to keep your nails neat and clean is to make sure they are short and cut properly with a nail clipper. Do you know someone that chews their fingernails? Sometimes people don't know that they are chewing on a piece of fingernail. This is not a very healthy habit. Sometimes your fingers will get sore and bleed from the chewing. Sometimes your fingernails are not very clean and they shouldn't be going in your mouth. That's why it's better to use a fingernail clipper to keep your fingernails short and neat.

Another way to keep your nails clean is to brush them, just like your teeth. Sometimes you can find a little brush, it looks like a toothbrush only a little bigger and it doesn't have a handle. This is called a nail brush. You can use a nail brush to scrub your fingernails and your toenails so that they are very clean.

Here's something fun to do. Gather up some old magazines. Cut out pictures that show clean and neat hair, teeth, nails, hands, and faces. Paste them on a blank piece of paper and you'll have a picture-perfect collage. Paste this collage up somewhere so you can see it when you're getting ready to go somewhere. It will remind you how important it is to look as good on the outside as you feel on the inside.

Wow, there's sure plenty of things to learn about grooming from head to toe. How will you ever remember everything? Practice makes perfect and every time you are polite to yourself, it will get easier. Remember these four important things:

1. Hair should be washed and combed. Long hair should be neat and tidy and away from your face so everyone can see your eyes.
2. Hands should be washed after messy activities and checked occasionally to be sure they're clean.
3. Teeth should be brushed and flossed to keep breath clean.
4. Fingernails should be short and neat and unchewed.

Chapter 3
Here and There, What to Wear: Rules For Dressing

When people first look at you, they look at your face. Another thing they notice about you is your clothes. If your clothes are sloppy and wrinkled, it tells people that you don't take good care of yourself and your things. Remember, the way you look tells people something about you. When you wear clean and neat clothes, you tell people you care about yourself and they should care about you too.

Keeping Clothes-Minded
When we're getting dressed in the morning, it's important to check and make sure our clothes are clean and neat. This is easier to do if we've put  them away properly in the first place! That means hanging up our clean clothes or putting them away neatly and putting our dirty clothes in the laundry and not on the floor.

Another way to show respect for ourselves is to take good care of our things. Did your parents ever say, "don't mess up your good clothes" or "go and change into your jeans to play outside?" That's because your good clothing is expensive and it's a lot of work to keep these clothes clean and make sure all the buttons and zippers work. If we wear our good clothes only for special activities, they will last longer and they won't get ripped or stained. Besides, play clothes are for playing and are much more comfortable than our good clothes.

What to Wear Where
Let's have a look in our closets and our drawers. Most of us have many clothes to choose from when we are deciding what to wear. Picking the right clothes for the right activity is important. It would not be very smart to wear your ski suit to the beach, would it? Can you imagine how funny you'd look if you wore your Halloween

costume to your grandma's for dinner? It's important to get it right when deciding what to wear!

Think about what you'll be doing each day when you are getting dressed. Pick the right clothes for the right occasion. And remember to take the time to change out of your good clothes and into your play clothes before you go outside!

Lace Me Up, Suzie
Don't forget, shoes are important too. So, make sure you choose the proper ones. Imagine how silly it would be to wear your beach sandals to gym class? What if you wore your slippers to the baseball game? If you wear the wrong shoes for the activity, you just might not be able to participate at all. After all, your beach sandals would go flying off at the gym, and in your slippers, you wouldn't be able to run very well so you probably wouldn't even get invited to play ball!

Sloppy Sue and Spiffy Sam can hardly wait. Today they are taking a school trip to the zoo and are having a picnic in the park. Plenty of walking and exercise. What about shoes? Sloppy Sue looks in her closet and tries to decide which shoes to choose. Can you help her decide? Here is a list of shoes in Sue's closet. What should she wear today?

Ballet slippers, beach sandals, hiking boots, party dress shoes, slippers or running shoes?

Yes, you are right! The running shoes will be comfortable and can be tied firmly to fit her feet. When you plan on doing a lot of walking you must respect your feet and keep them in good shape. If you wear the wrong shoes, your feet will hurt, and you won't be able to walk tall.

Remember too, to take care of your shoes. The laces in your shoes need to be in good repair without tears and tied up just right, not too loose and not too tight. If your shoes are unlaced, you could even trip and get hurt! You can also take care of your shoes by keeping them clean; wipe off scuff marks and spray off mud or sand after a day of play. And remember to wipe your feet on the mat before you walk into someone's house!

Belts, Buckles, Barrettes, and Baubles

Have you ever heard someone say, "it's the little things that count?" Sometimes we have to think about "accessories" too. Accessories are extra things, not really clothing, but they are sometimes necessary to make our appearance more "appropriate" for the activity we are doing.

Here are some examples of accessories, think about where you might need them:

- A Raincoat
- Sunglasses
- A beach bag
- An umbrella
- A rain hat
- A knapsack
- A watch
- Jewelry
- A purse or wallet
- Rubber Boots

Accessories are also important because they make our lives easier. Close your eyes and picture yourself packing up to go to the beach. Put all your towels, sandals, toys, sunscreen, and snacks in a beach bag or carry them under your arms or hooked on your fingers. What looks easier? You've got it. We would drop most everything without our beach bag.

Looking good from head to toe is important, and that means paying attention to our clothes, shoes, and accessories, and remembering to keep neat and clean. Here are the four things to remember:

1. Clothes should be neat and tidy with no tears or rips or spaghetti stains. Don't forget, wrinkled clothing makes you look lazy and sloppy.
2. Wear the right clothing. Think about what you'll be doing today and make sure you are wearing the right thing.
3. Shoes need to be clean and in good repair. Please remember to think about the proper shoes to wear for each activity.
4. Accessories are extra little things that you bring with you or they can be items you put on before you leave the house. Remember, sometimes it is the little things that count.

This poem might help you remember how "appropriate clothing" is important.

We're going to the beach to play in the sand
With our good manners hand in hand,
we know we want to have a ball
So maybe we will stop at the mall.
We'll trade our jeans and rubber boots
for playful hats and bathing suits.
We'll bring along a towel and you,
Don't forget your sandals too!

Here's an idea, why don't you get a pencil and paper and write a poem about what to wear when you're going to a restaurant or someone's house for dinner.

Chapter 4
Deportment is Important: Sitting, Standing, and Walking

Do you know what "deportment" is? Deportment means how you carry yourself; how you walk or sit or stand. If you have a good deportment that means you carry yourself in a polite way that shows the world you are confident about who you are, how you look, and what you have to say.

Let's see what our friends Sloppy Sue and Spiffy Sam are doing right now. Oh no, I think I see Sloppy Sue. She is at the table all slouched down in her chair. She has her feet on the furniture and a sad look on her face. Not like Spiffy Sam, he's sitting straight up at the table with his feet on the floor and his hands in his lap. He is smiling and looks like he's happy. Who would you like to sit beside?

Polite Posture
How we sit and stand, and walk is called posture. I'm sure your parents or teachers have told you to "stand up straight." Good posture shows that we feel good about ourselves, that we are interested in what is going on around us, and that we are confident. It is always important to have our back's straight. This not only makes us taller, but it makes us look like we are sure of ourselves. Slouching shows others that we're not confident in ourselves, so we're hunching over and trying to cover ourselves up.

It can also give people the message that we aren't interested in what they're saying, or that we're bored or tired. The other problem with slouching is that it makes it hard for people to see our faces and hear what we're saying. If we like ourselves, we want people to see us and hear us. That's showing ourselves respect – and them too!

Sitting Pretty
When we sit, we need to remember to keep our backs straight and our feet flat on the floor. We try not to put our feet on the

furniture; it gets the furniture dirty and it also makes it hard for us to have good posture. And don't lean too far back on the chair – you might fall over!

Ouch, what a grouch! That's what I think when I see Sloppy Sue, who's always slouching. Why don't you try it? Find a chair and sit all slouched over and not straight in your chair. It doesn't feel very good, does it? Now try sitting straight. There, that's much better.

Remember, sitting pretty shows people that you respect them, and their furniture, and yourself.

Standing Tall
When we stand, we need to keep our shoulders back and our feet flat on the ground. You can leave your arms at your sides or hold your hands together in front of you, but it's a good idea not to cross them in front of you – that gives people the idea that you are stubborn or angry. Better to leave your arms at your sides. And don't hold them behind your back – it looks like you're hiding something!

Let's try this. Look in the mirror and practice good posture. First, stand all slouched with your head and shoulders down. Then stand up straight and tall. See the difference? When you stand tall you look confident and people can see your smiling face. Now try slouching again and say something out loud. Did you notice how hard it is to hear yourself? It would be really hard for someone else to hear you.

It's especially important to stand up straight or sit up straight when you're talking to people. Good posture helps you breathe better so your voice is crisp and clear, and everyone can hear what you're saying.

Walk the Straight and Narrow
Did someone ever tell you to "pick up your feet" when you walk?

Or maybe they said "put your shoulders back" and "hold your head up" or "don't swing your arms when you walk." That's because posture is important when you are walking too.

Clomp, clomp, shuffle, shuffle…. What's that noise? I think it's Sloppy Sue coming down the hall. If only she'd pick up her feet, she'd probably get places much quicker and feel much better about herself.

Let's go back to the mirror. Try walking past it just like Sloppy Sue. First, walk really fast and swing your arms. See how silly it looks? It would be easy to accidentally hit someone as you were passing by. Now try walking really slowly and don't lift your heels as you walk. See how your feet drag and make a shuffling sound? How do you think walking like this makes you look? That's right! Tired and lazy.

The proper way to walk is standing straight with your arms loosely by your sides, but not swinging. You should pick up your feet and put your heels down first. Some other things to remember:

- Don't walk with your hands in your pockets.
- Hold your head up.
- Keep your eyes forward.

That's right, just like Spiffy Sam would do.
When you feel great about yourself, you sit up straight, stand tall, and walk with confidence. You always keep your head up high and a bright smile on your face, and you never slouch. Remember:

1. Sit with your feet flat on the ground and your back straight. Don't put your feet up on the furniture.
2. Stand straight and tall with your head up so people can see your face.

3. Walk with your arms at your sides and remember to lift your feet and not shuffle.

Spiffy Sam wants to share a poem with you. He hopes this will help you to remember that deportment is important.

If I stand straight and tall and proud,
I'm telling people right out loud
That I feel great and
I can't wait to go outside and celebrate.
I pick up my feet, not shuffling along;
It's important to show I'm happy to belong.
As lunchtime arrives, I'm ready to eat.
I sit up straight, and tidy and neat,
feet on the floor, not slouching at all,
confident, proud and having a ball.

Chapter 5
Decorum Forum: Acting Appropriately

It's great to be well-groomed so we look good on the outside and it's also important to feel good on the inside because this shows we have self-respect. If we want other people to know we respect them too, we have to think about how we act. Acting appropriately is called "decorum." When we practice good manners, we show others all the things we've learned so far, that we feel good on the inside, that we look good on the outside, that we carry ourselves with confidence. There are special rules for decorum depending on where you are and who you're with, but some things are true in every situation.

Lose the "Tude", Dude

The way you act says a lot about the way you feel about yourself inside. When you smile and stand straight and speak clearly, you show a "positive attitude."

When you slouch or mumble your words, you show a "bad attitude." People who have "positive attitudes" feel good about themselves and about other people. They don't expect people to be perfect, they listen, and they are interested in what other people have to tell them. They are also people who like to try new things. Have you ever played games with someone like this? A person with a positive attitude can be a lot of fun!

Remember how we said that both Sloppy Sue and Spiffy Sam are special, but they are also different? That's because Spiffy Sam understands that even though he looks good, he also has to act properly. Spiffy Sam has a positive attitude and Sloppy Sue has a lazy, impolite attitude. It's important to have a positive attitude because the way you act goes hand in hand with how you look.

The Nose Knows

Achoo! What would you do if you had to cough or had to sneeze? Well, I'm sure you've heard adults tell you to "cover your mouth" or "use a tissue." That's because coughing and sneezing spreads germs that make other people sick. When you cover up your mouth or use a tissue to blow your nose, you're keeping your germs to yourself!

Sometimes, when your nose gets full or itchy, you need to blow your nose. And everyone knows you use a tissue for that. Your finger will not do! It's really important to remember that other people do not want to see what's inside your nose, just like you wouldn't want to see inside anyone else's. Using a tissue is a way to be polite to other people. And they'll like you a lot better for it.

Another thing to remember is never, never to wipe your hands on your clothes, no matter what is on them. If you can't find a tissue, go to the washroom and use toilet paper. Having dirty stuff all over your clothes tells people you are sloppy and lazy and it's not very nice for them to look at. Remember, keeping clean and neat is a way to show respect not only for other people but for yourself too!

Good Habits Are Hard to Find

Politeness is all about acting on the outside the way we feel on the inside. One way to practice good manners all the time is to develop good habits. Do you know what a habit is? A habit is something we do over and over without thinking. If we try to always practice our manners, we will soon have good habits and we'll do the polite thing without even thinking about it.

Say out loud the good habits and the bad habits in the list below. Think about what Sloppy Sue or Spiffy Sam would do.

- Brushing your teeth
- Chew gum loudly
- Never using dental floss
- Shampooing your hair

- Taking a bath
- Getting all dirty
- Having dirty fingernails
- Tidying your room
- Wearing wrinkle-free clothes
- Leaving your clothes on the floor

Maybe you can think of some other bad habits. If you can, say them out loud and then say to yourself, "I'm going to try very hard not to have these bad habits anymore!"

Congratulations, now you know all about decorum. It's great to see you will soon have good habits and remember the rules:

1. A positive attitude will influence the way you act and make you a pleasant person to be around.
2. Always use a tissue when you need to blow your nose or when you sneeze. Never use your fingers or your clothes.
3. Develop good habits by practicing them every day.

So, don't forget that even though you show care and consideration by how you look you also have to show care and consideration by how you act.

Chapter 6
Even When They Can't See You: Telephone and Internet Manners

We've learned a lot about the way we feel on the inside and how that reflects on the outside. But it's also important to remember deportment and decorum when people can't see us. What are some situations where we are interacting with people, but they can't see us? That's right. When we talk on the phone or through email!

Hello, Hello is Anybody There?
Why do you think it's important to be polite when you're talking on the phone? That's because being polite is a way of showing respect for others and for yourself. Just like there are rules for every situation, there are special rules for being polite on the telephone. Try to remember these things when you are talking on the phone.

1. Speak calmly and clearly.
2. Say hello and say your name.
3. Ask for the person for whom you are calling. Remember to say please.
4. If they're not home, leave a message.
5. Say thank you and goodbye. Hang up gently.

It's important to remember all the things we've learned so far, but the most important thing is your attitude. Even if people can't see your face, they can tell what kind of attitude you have and the mood you're in just by the sound of your voice.

Someone's Calling Me
When you hear the phone ringing, it's important to try to answer it as quickly as possible. It's never polite to keep people waiting, and it's not polite to wait for someone else to answer the phone either.

Generally, whoever is closest should always answer the phone. When you're answering the phone, the same rules apply as when you are phoning someone else but there are three other things to remember:

1. If the call is for you, have a conversation but try not to talk too long in case someone else needs the phone.
2. If the call is for someone else, gently put down the phone and go get the person. Take a message if the person is not home.
3. Don't ever tell someone your parents are not home. It's better to say, "They can't come to the phone right now, may I take a message."

Let's practice. Telephone an adult you know and tell them you are practicing your telephone manners and ask them to telephone you back. Try to remember all the rules for answering the telephone.

There are a lot of rules to remember about the telephone. Ask your parents if you can make a list of things to remember and stick it by the telephone to remind you how to be polite until you have all the rules memorized.

I'd Like to Leave a Message, Please
What happens at your house when you're not home and someone telephones for you? I bet you'd be happy to get a message that someone called, right? And it sure would be nice to know who they were and what they wanted. Getting messages right is important. This shows respect for the person who telephoned and respect for the person getting the message.

Here are four questions you need to ask when you take a message:

1. Who called?
2. Who did they call for?
3. What time did they call?

4. What was the reason for the call?

Practice taking messages by asking a friend to pretend they're calling. See if you can remember to get the questions right without looking at the list!

If you get messages right, people never need to call back to figure out what's going on. And remember, always write down your name so the person getting the message knows to take the call!

<u>Oh No, I'm Caught in the Net!</u>
Email is a way that your friends can call you without using a telephone and send you notes or letters, even invitations, without using the regular mail. Computers and the Internet are very interesting and fun to use. It's important to remember some rules though, or you could get caught in an inter "net."

The rules for email are a lot like the rules for the phone, except that you're writing instead of talking. Take a look.

1. Make sure you sign your name so the person getting your email knows who sent it.
2. Make sure you write down who the message is for because sometimes more than one person shares an email address.
3. Answer your email as soon as you can. It's rude to keep people waiting.
4. If you don't hear back from someone right away, don't send the message again. Once is enough.

Spiffy Sam sends emails to all his friends and always remembers to address the emails properly. Sloppy Sue is pleasantly surprised to receive Sam's email. She often complains that no-one ever sends her any mail, but that's because she is sometimes lazy about writing people back. You have to give to receive! This is true for the phone, too.

Don't "Talk" to Strangers
Remember when you were young, and your parents told you not to talk to strangers? Well, you shouldn't talk to strangers on the Internet either. Never go to a chat room without your parents' supervision because you don't know who the other people in the chat room are. And never give out personal information like your name, age, address, telephone number, or the school you attend. If someone you don't know sends you an email, tell your parents right away. Don't talk to strangers even if you think it would be fun because it's not safe. The internet can be lots of fun and there are lots of very interesting things to see and learn but, just like when we're out and about in the world, we have to be careful.

The important things to remember about the phone and Internet etiquette are:

1. Speak clearly and slowly on the telephone. Make sure you say your name.
2. If you are taking a message, make sure to get all the important information, like who called, when they called and who they called for.
3. When you are sending emails, make sure you address them properly.
4. Never talk to strangers, not on the phone, and not on the Internet.

And don't forget, how you feel on the inside shows on the outside. Even if people can't see you – they can still hear your voice and read your ideas and guess how you are feeling.

Conclusion
Courtesy Becomes Me

So, what do you think would happen if Sloppy Sue spent a lot of time with Spiffy Sam and followed his example? That's right, it wouldn't take long before she has good habits too and then we could call her "Snazzy Sue." How about you? Let's see if you can be a Spiffy Sam and remember how to be polite because courtesy becomes you. When you treat yourself with respect, that's called self-respect and shows other people that you have care and consideration for yourself. Be proud to be who you are and don't be too hard on yourself if you make a mistake because no-one is perfect. We have to respect each other and remember that everyone has something that makes them special.

Well, it looks like you've been paying attention and you know all about manners now. Just for fun, let's take a quiz and see how much you remember about showing and respect for yourself and others.

Take the quiz on the next page. Say out loud if the statement is true or false. Then turn to the very last page and check how many of the questions you answered correctly.

Take the Quiz

1. Sometimes if okay to have a "mop-top" if you're tired and really busy.

2. If someone telephones for your brother and he isn't in the same room as the telephone, you should just yell for him to come and get the phone.

3. Chewing gum and popping bubbles is fun and doesn't bother other people.

4. When you're a guest at someone else's house, it's okay to forget your manners.

5. It's important to wear "appropriate" clothing for special occasions; it's a way of showing self- respect.

6. Slouching when you sit and dragging your feet when you walk tells others you are confident and full of energy.

7. When you send an email, you don't need to sign your name.

8. You should always brush your teeth in the morning and before bed.

9. Chewing your nails keeps them short and neat.

10. It's okay to wear a hat at the dinner table if you wear it backwards.

Let's see how you did, see the answers on the next page!

Answers

1. False
2. False
3. False
4. False
5. True
6. False
7. False
8. True
9. False
10. False

www.ingramcontent.com/pod-product-compliance
Lightning Source LLC
LaVergne TN
LVHW010035070426
835510LV00006B/133